FYI

Send-Home Letters
about
God's Children
to
PARENTS

Marti Beuschlein

Illustrated by Becky Radtke

CPH
SAINT LOUIS

"For my family life mentors, my friends—Beth Innes and Patti Hoffman"

For families of young children who valiantly struggle in an uncertain world to raise their children so they may "grow in the grace and knowledge of our Lord and Savior Jesus Christ" (2 Peter 3:18)

Scripture quotations, unless otherwise indicated, are taken from the HOLY BIBLE, NEW INTERNATIONAL VERSION®. NIV®. Copyright © 1973, 1978, 1984 by International Bible Society. Used by permission of Zondervan Publishing House. All rights reserved.

Text copyright © 2000 Martha Beuschlein
Illustrations copyright © 2000 Concordia Publishing House

Published by Concordia Publishing House
3558 S. Jefferson Avenue, St. Louis, MO 63118–3968
Manufactured in the United States of America

1   2   3   4   5   6   7   8   9   10   09   08   07   06   05   04   03   02   01   00

Contents

Introduction

Growing and Learning —Chapter One 7

Powerful Play
Sleep Tight—God Is Watching over You
Separation
Validating Children's Feelings

15 Chapter Two— Guiding Behavior

The Ten-Letter Word—Discipline
Using Words for Feelings
Empowering Children to Make Decisions
Consequences of Our Actions
Problem Solving

Special Times —Chapter Three 27

Take that Baby Back
Why Is the Moving Van in Front of Our House?
Waiting for Baby Jesus
Grandpa Died
Holidays, Celebrations, and Children

39 Chapter Four— Family Fun

Are We There Yet?
Summer Time Fun
Take a Hike

At School —Chapter Five 47

School Days—A New Beginning
What Did You Do in School Today?
See What I Made
Explore, Experiment, Create
Surf and Turf—Sand and Water Play
Math—More Than Counting to Ten
Developmentally Appropriate
Hands-on-Learning

INTRODUCTION

Dear friends of young children,

This book was written to be shared with teachers and families of young children, for we are "... members of one body, and sharers together in the promise in Christ Jesus" (Ephesians 3:6). As "sharers together in the promise," our goal is to proclaim the Good News to young children so that they may "grow in the grace and knowledge of our Lord and Savior Jesus Christ" (2 Peter 3:18).

It is with pleasure that I share some of what I have learned during 40+ years of teaching and/or administering programs for young children. All of the stories are real—either from my teaching or parenting experiences (four sons and seven grandsons). I know that you desire to support and assist families in any possible way. I also know how difficult it is to find time to specifically address concerns and questions.

While there is no substitute for one-on-one communication, these letters will help you meet the needs of families. Give one to a parent who has a question or concern, or publish them as a regular feature in your newsletter.

Here are some ways to personalize the letters:

- ATTACH A SCHEDULE OF AVAILABLE PROGRAMS FOR FAMILIES TO ATTEND CONCERNING THE ISSUE ADDRESSED IN THE LETTER.

- PROVIDE A RESOURCE LIST OF BOOKS, VIDEOS, OR OTHER BOOKLETS AS ADDITIONAL RESOURCES. ARTICLES CUT OUT FROM MAGAZINES AND PERIODICALS CAN ALSO BE ATTACHED OR MADE AVAILABLE.

- ADD COPIES OF PHOTOS ILLUSTRATING ACTIVITIES IN THE CLASSROOM.

This book is organized into the following chapters:

CHAPTER ONE—GROWING AND LEARNING

Use these letters to answer parent questions concerning everyday occurrences such as "How do I get my child to stay in her own bed?" When parents are questioning the value of play in your classroom, print the letter "Powerful Play" in a newsletter to all families.

CHAPTER TWO—GUIDING BEHAVIOR

Letters in this chapter can be used at various times during the year as occasions arise. They can also be used as a series on "Guiding Behavior" in your monthly newsletters.

CHAPTER THREE—SPECIAL TIMES

"How do I tell my child her nana died?" Pull out "Grandpa Died" and give it to parents facing this situation. The holiday letters can be sent home with the children before a holiday or celebration.

CHAPTER FOUR—FAMILY FUN

Use these letters to suggest appropriate activities for your families to do together. They can be used as part of a series, or photocopied on an individual basis.

CHAPTER FIVE—AT SCHOOL

This chapter was designed to help you answer frequently asked questions concerning activities in the classroom and the reason for doing them.

I pray that God will bless you in your ministry to young children and their families, and that these reproducible letters will be an effective tool for you.

Marti Beuschlein

Chapter One
GROWING AND LEARNING

POWERFUL PLAY

by Marti Beuschlein

Be happy, young man, while you are young, and let your heart give you joy in the days of your youth.
(Ecclesiastes 11:9)

The phrase "they are just playing" is often heard among conversations of teachers and parents. Frequently, play appears to adults—especially those who do not value play for themselves—as aimless puttering about with paints, toys, or blocks. However, God in His infinite wisdom created children not only to enjoy play, but to learn through the process of playing.

For the young child play is:

o DISCOVERING AND EXPLORING

o BUILDING SELF-CONFIDENCE

o TESTING NEW IDEAS OR STRATEGIES

o MAKING SENSE OF GOD'S WORLD

o TAKING RISKS

o ACTIVE LEARNING WITH "HANDS-ON" EXPERIENCES

o MAKING DECISIONS AND CHOICES

o BUILDING VERBAL SKILLS

o INTERACTING AND BUILDING RELATIONSHIPS

o DEVELOPING POSITIVE CHRIST-CENTERED ATTITUDES

o THE PRIMARY MEANS BY WHICH CHILDREN LEARN

o FUN!!

At home ...

- PROVIDE A "PLAY-SPACE" THAT HAS AMPLE ROOM FOR TOYS AND STORAGE. THE TOYS AND PLAY SPACE DO NOT NEED TO BE LARGE AND ELABORATE. COLORFUL PLASTIC CRATES AND A CORNER OF A BEDROOM OR FAMILY ROOM IS SUFFICIENT.

- YOUNG CHILDREN LOVE TO PLAY WITH REAL ITEMS SUCH AS ADULT CLOTHING, POTS AND PANS, PLASTIC DISHES, PURSES, BRIEFCASES, AND TELEPHONES. KEEP SAFETY IN MIND AS YOU PROVIDE PLAY PROPS FOR YOUR CHILDREN.

- GIVE CHILDREN TIME — TIME TO PLAY AND TO COMPLETE A PLAY SCENARIO. SET A KITCHEN TIMER TO INDICATE WHEN IT IS TIME TO STOP PLAYING AND PICK UP TOYS. A FIVE-MINUTE WARNING GIVES CHILDREN AN OPPORTUNITY TO BRING THEIR PLAY TO A CLOSE.

- PLAY WITH YOUR CHILDREN. HAVE A TEA PARTY. BUILD A BLOCK STRUCTURE. DRESS UP AND DANCE TO MUSIC. CREATE NEW ENVIRONMENTS SUCH AS A CHURCH, AN AIRPLANE OR TRAIN INTERIOR, A DOCTOR'S OFFICE, OR A FLORIST. ENCOURAGE YOUR CHILDREN TO USE THEIR IMAGINATIONS OR SIMPLE PROPS WHEN THEY PRETEND.

Pretend Airplane

Build a pretend airplane with your children. Put several chairs in a row to resemble the interior of an airplane. Pack duffel bags, old purses, or briefcases to take on the "trip." Serve snacks on TV trays or paper plates. Take turns playing flight attendant. This is an excellent way to introduce a first-time airplane ride to your children. Remind your children that God watches over them and takes care of them no matter where they are.

I tried to teach my child from books—
He only gave me puzzled looks.
I tried to teach my child with words—
They passed him by, often unheard.
Despairingly I turned aside,
"How shall I teach this child?" I cried.
Into my hand he put the key—
"Come," he said, "and play with me."

Author unknown

Prayer

Heavenly Father, thank You for the gift of (name your children). Help me to understand them and to guide their play so that they may continue to grow as loving children in our Lord and Savior Jesus Christ. Amen.

Sleep Tight—God Is Watching Over You

by Marti Beuschlein

I will lie down and sleep in peace, for You alone O LORD, make me dwell in safety.
(Psalm 4:8)

Looking at your children—curled up, nestled in bed, and peacefully sleeping—is a sight to behold and cherish. Children need rest and sleep. Parents need children to rest and sleep so that they themselves can slumber and be refreshed. Yet, bedtime can be a difficult time for parents as well as children.

Bedtime Routine

Establish a bedtime routine and use it daily. Young children like to know what will happen next and respond well to routines. Sample routine:

o BATH WITH PLENTY OF TIME FOR WATER PLAY

o RUB DOWN AND DRY OFF WITH A FLUFFY TOWEL AND ONE-ON-ONE CONVERSATION

o STORY TIME—READ A BOOK WHILE LYING IN BED, OR SITTING IN A ROCKER OR A BIG COMFY CHAIR

o TUCK INTO BED

o SAY PRAYERS

o HUGS AND KISSES

o TURN OFF THE LIGHT AND LEAVE.

Whatever bedtime routine you establish, make sure it meets the needs of you, your children, and your family. Read a Bible story to your children each night as part of your bedtime routine. This is a great opportunity to nurture your children's faith and to talk about Jesus' love, and what it means for you and your family.

Nightmares

Nightmares are common and normal for children ages three to five. In a dark room, shadows become scary animals and squeaky floors become monster noises.

Follow these guidelines to help alleviate fears and assure children:

o REMIND THEM THAT GOD WATCHES OVER US WHILE WE SLEEP. REPEAT THE BIBLE VERSE ABOVE.

o SAY A PRAYER ASKING FOR GOD'S PROTECTION.

o SIT FOR AWHILE AFTER BAD DREAMS TO ASSURE CHILDREN THAT THEY ARE SAFE.

o SPRAY AWAY THE "BAD MONSTERS" WITH "MONSTER SPRAY" (A SPRAY BOTTLE FILLED WITH WATER).

o TURN ON A NIGHT-LIGHT.

If keeping your children in bed is a struggle, ask yourself these questions:

o IS THE BEDTIME ROUTINE TOO STIMULATING? IS THERE ROWDY PLAY RATHER THAN QUIET DOWN-TIME BEFORE BED? (A QUIET TIME PROVIDES AN OPPORTUNITY FOR FAMILY DEVOTIONS AND PRAYER.)

o ARE YOUR CHILDREN WATCHING INAPPROPRIATE, VIOLENT, OR SCARY TELEVISION PROGRAMS BEFORE BED?

o HAVE ALL OF YOUR CHILDREN'S NEEDS BEEN MET, SUCH AS ONE LAST DRINK, GOING POTTY, OR READING A STORY? (BY MEETING THESE NEEDS BEFORE TUCKING YOUR CHILD IN BED, YOU TAKE AWAY THE EXCUSES. BE FIRM AND SAY, "YOU HAD A DRINK, A STORY, AND PLENTY OF HUGS AND KISSES. IT IS TIME TO GO TO SLEEP. GOODNIGHT.")

o ARE YOUR CHILDREN REALLY TIRED AND READY FOR SLEEP? (TAKE A GOOD LOOK AT THEIR DAILY ROUTINES. IS NAPTIME TOO LONG OR TOO LATE IN THE DAY? YOU MAY NEED TO MOVE NAPTIME OR BEDTIME TO EARLIER OR LATER IN THE DAY.)

Exceptions to the Rules

Children need reassurance, warmth, and love when they are sick, frightened, or lonely. Extra time and care might be needed at these times.

Jon, Tim, Tom, and Peter have fond memories of Saturday mornings with all four boys and Mom and Dad tucked in bed chatting together, along with some tumbling and jumping. Sometimes they read the paper together or watched cartoons. When 26-year-old Peter still lived at home and worked late hours, he would lie at the foot of our bed and watch a favorite TV program before going to bed. Create some of these same memories for your children.

Prayer

Heavenly Father, help my family feel secure in Your loving and protective care while we sleep. Awake us with refreshment and newness so that we may serve You in Your kingdom. In Jesus' name. Amen.
Use this new version of an old prayer:

Now I lay me down to sleep,
I pray the Lord
His watch to keep.
Angels guard me till I wake.
I thank the Lord
as morning breaks.

SEPARATION

by Marti Beuschlein

"Peace I leave with you; My peace I give you. I do not give to you as the world gives. Do not let your hearts be troubled and do not be afraid." (John 14:27)

I wept often during the first two days of a trip to London. It was the first time that I had visited a foreign country without my husband. I felt the tug of separation in my body and soul. After a long distance phone call, my anxiety and fears subsided.

o WE OFTEN FEAR THE UNKNOWN—WHAT WILL HAPPEN TO ME IN THIS NEW PLACE? HOW WILL THE PEOPLE TREAT ME? WILL I DO SOMETHING SILLY TO MAKE PEOPLE LAUGH AT ME? AM I SAFE HERE?

o WE ARE ANXIOUS ABOUT THE ONES WE LEFT BEHIND. WHAT ARE THEY DOING WITHOUT ME? WHERE ARE THEY?

o WE MISS THE COMFORTS OF OUR OWN PLACE AND SPACE. I DON'T KNOW WHERE TO PUT MY COAT. WHERE IS THE BATHROOM? WHAT KIND OF FOOD WILL I EAT HERE?

Young children experience the same anxieties and fears as adults; however, they do not have the resources and cognitive development to deal with their responses to fear. They lose their sense of security. To make matters worse, children experience anxiety when separated from the people who help them feel secure.

Young children who react to separation will do so in various ways. They may do anything from crying hysterically and throwing a tantrum, to retreating quietly under a table to pout. Sometimes children may react to separation immediately or delay their reaction for weeks. The reaction may last for a few minutes, a few hours, or several days.

Support & Trust

Adults need to personally deal with their own separation issues before helping young children.

Often, adults do not take separation anxiety seriously because separation is also painful for them. Although it is easier to avoid dealing with issues related to separation, avoiding them may create an even greater risk.

Learning to deal with separation together can strengthen family trust and support. Unsuccessful and glossed-over separation experiences threaten trust and family support; it is not worth it to deny or avoid separation.

Ask God to give you guidance and strength to deal with it openly and with a positive attitude.

Honesty and Trust

In order to protect children, adults often avoid telling the truth, making comments such as "the shot won't hurt" or "I'll be right back." The old adage "what they don't know won't hurt them" is precisely what *does* hurt them.

Be honest. Tell children the simple truth in terms and language they can understand. Tell them that you are leaving but you will be back to pick them up. Pray with them, asking Jesus to calm their fears.

Listen to your children as they tell you about their feelings. Deal with their reactions and reassure them of your love and support, as well as God's love for them.

Our role as adults is to assist children in their life journey and equip them to meet new challenges successfully. Building a sense of trust in these early years will set the foundation for trusting in God who cares for all of our needs—especially our need for a Savior.

Prayer

Dear Lord, give me the wisdom to recognize opportunities for building a sense of trust in my children.
Help them to know that they can trust You to care for every need.
Help me to be aware of Your presence and bless my efforts to ease the separation experiences of my children. In Your name.
Amen.

Chapter Two GUIDING BEHAVIOR

THE TEN-LETTER WORD: DISCIPLINE

by Marti Beuschlein

Discipline your son, and he will give you peace; he will bring delight to your soul.
(Proverbs 29:17)

The Bible tells us to discipline our children. It also states that a disciplined child will bring peace and delight to our soul.

But how do we discipline our children in a God-pleasing way? What can we do that really works?

Discipline is not punishment. The goal of *punishment* is to make children pay for their misbehavior and to be afraid to repeat any behavior that results in pain. The goal of *discipline* is to help children develop the behaviors necessary for successful living.

The role of adults is to help children develop habits of discipline that create self-discipline. Young children are in the process of growing and learning about themselves and their relationships with others—peers, siblings, and adults. Keep in mind that positive and constructive discipline preserves and enhances feelings of confidence.

Children misbehave for a variety of reasons. They may be frustrated or discouraged.

Sometimes children are simply angry at themselves or others; sometimes they are just mad at the world in general. (Be honest; as adults we also have these same feelings at times.) Children may also behave badly when they are afraid of the dark, loud noises, threats, or punishment.

To discipline means to teach children right from wrong. Discipline means setting limits and sound boundaries. Discipline means loving and trusting children. Discipline means consistency in enforcing limits and rules.

Discipline requires forgiveness—dislike the sin, but love and forgive the sinner. Look to God for help in following His model of love and forgiveness.

Give children a balance of:

o LOVE—ACCEPT, TRUST, AND UNDERSTAND YOUR CHILDREN.

o RESPECT—VALUE THEM AS UNIQUE INDIVIDUALS, CREATED BY GOD.

o ORDER—BE FIRM AND USE REASONABLE CONTROL TO CREATE A WARM AND SAFE ENVIRONMENT.

o FAIRNESS—DISCIPLINE EQUALLY AND ADAPT METHODS TO MEET THE TEMPERAMENT OF INDIVIDUAL CHILDREN.

Ways to Guide Children toward Acceptable Behavior

o DISCIPLINE BEFORE YOU HAVE REACHED THE END OF YOUR ROPE AND PATIENCE.

o LET YOUR CHILDREN KNOW THAT YOU LOVE THEM AND THAT IT IS THE BAD BEHAVIOR THAT YOU DO NOT ACCEPT.

o KEEP RULES AND LIMITS SIMPLE, USING WORDS THAT CHILDREN CAN UNDERSTAND AND COMPREHEND.

o GIVE CHILDREN CHOICES. BE SURE THAT THE CHOICES ARE AGE-APPROPRIATE FOR THEM AND ACCEPTABLE TO YOU.

o BE CONSISTENT. CONSISTENCY IS SOMETIMES DIFFICULT, BUT PAYS OFF IN THE LONG RUN.

o PRAISE GOOD BEHAVIOR.

o MODEL SELF-DISCIPLINE.

Prayer

Dear Jesus, it was You who, out of love, commanded us to discipline our children. Forgive me for the times that I have done this in anger or frustration. Give me wisdom and help me find loving ways to discipline so that my children might experience Your love and forgivness through me.
Amen.

Using Words for Feelings

by Marti Beuschlein

A word aptly spoken is like apples of gold in settings of silver. (Proverbs 25:11)

Adults model acceptable behavior by the way we act and speak. The words we use, the tone of voice we maintain, and our demeanor have great impact. The words we use can help children understand their feelings and help them to express themselves to their peers.

Talking with Children

- State expectations using positive language. Say "Chairs are for sitting" rather than "Don't stand on the chair."

- Avoid using negative language. Get rid of "good/bad, nice/naughty." Instead use "You have learned to put away your toys."

- Be specific when making requests. Use "Put on your socks and then your shoes" rather than "Get dressed."

- Be pleasant instead of shouting or scolding. Say "Please put the truck in the toy box" rather than "Pick up these toys right now."

- Use non-verbal language. Show approval or disapproval through a touch, a smile, or a nod.

- Avoid making threats, especially ones you cannot carry out (e.g. "You're not going to child care if you don't stop that").

- Praise or disapprove of the action—never the children. "You brushed your teeth very well." "I don't like what you did. That hurt your brother when you hit him."

- Accept your children's feelings and address their behavior. "I know you're angry, but I can't let you throw toys."

Helping Children Use Words for Feelings

o ENCOURAGE CHILDREN TO USE WORDS INSTEAD OF ACTIONS TO TELL OTHERS HOW THEY FEEL.

"It's **OK** to be angry. Tell Jake how angry you are."

"Tell Kasey you do not like it when he hits you."

"You need to use words instead of biting."

"I know that you are mad when Vicki calls you names. Tell Vicki how that makes you feel."

o MODEL USING LANGUAGE TO EXPRESS FEELINGS WHEN YOU ARE UPSET.

"I worry when you jump from that high table. That is not safe. I am afraid you will get hurt."

"I am angry about this mess. I need to calm down and then we will talk about it."

"When I see all these toys on the floor, I am concerned that someone will step on them."

"I know you are mad at Rhonda, but I can't let you hit her."

Focusing on Feelings

Focus on feelings. Help children consider their feelings and learn to value their actions.

"I'll bet you feel proud that you buttoned your shirt."
"You are so excited that you can put that puzzle together."

Prayer

Dear Lord, help me to teach my children that they can come to You in prayer, pouring their feelings out to You. Help me to model speaking my feelings to my children so that they learn to use words instead of actions. I depend upon Your loving grace. Amen.

EMPOWERING CHILDREN TO MAKE DECISIONS

by Marti Beuschlein

"Give your servant a discerning heart ... to distinguish between right and wrong." (1 Kings 3:9)

My son **Tom** told me that when he was a teenager he was confronted with making many choices; whether to hang out with a group that did drugs or one that didn't. How do we help our children make the right choices?

First we pray that **God** will give us **His** wisdom and guidance. Then we begin to empower our children to make decisions when they are very young. Making small choices prepares them for the bigger ones that come later in their life journey.

What Shall I Wear?

- LAY OUT DIFFERENT OUTFITS AND GIVE YOUR CHILDREN THE CHOICE. "WHICH OUTFIT WOULD YOU LIKE TO WEAR TO SCHOOL?" "YOU CHOSE WELL. DO YOU LIKE THAT COLOR?"

- WHEN BUYING NEW CLOTHES, TAKE CHILDREN ALONG AND LET THEM MAKE SELECTIONS FROM SEVERAL YOU HAVE CHOSEN WITHIN YOUR PRICE RANGE AND THEIR CORRECT SIZE.

Family Meetings

- HAVE FAMILY MEETINGS AND ALLOW YOUR CHILDREN TO VOTE ON FAMILY DECISIONS. MAKE SURE. THEY ALSO KNOW THAT THEY HAVE THE RIGHT TO CALL A FAMILY MEETING.

- GIVE CHILDREN A CHOICE REGARDING FAMILY VACATIONS. HAVE BROCHURES AND SEVERAL OPTIONS AVAILABLE.

- LISTEN TO CHILDREN. IF WHAT THEY ARE ASKING IS INAPPROPRIATE, COME UP WITH APPROPRIATE OPTIONS AS CHOICES. "THAT IDEA IS NOT APPROPRIATE FOR OUR FAMILY, BUT WE COULD DO _____ OR _____. WHICH WOULD YOU PREFER?"

- "TOMORROW IS SATURDAY. SHALL WE HAVE A PICNIC OR GO TO THE ZOO?" MAKE THE DECISION THE NIGHT BEFORE AND INCLUDE THEM IN THE PREPARATIONS. "EVERYONE NEEDS TO HELP. WHO WANTS TO GET THE PICNIC BASKET OUT OF STORAGE?" PROVIDE A LIST OF TASKS, THEN GIVE A CHOICE OF WHICH THEY WILL DO.

- BEGIN WITH PRAYER, ASKING GOD TO HELP YOU MAKE DECISIONS THAT SHOW HIS LOVE AND ARE PLEASING TO HIM.

- END WITH PRAYER, THANKING AND PRAISING GOD FOR HIS GOODNESS AND FAITHFULNESS.

Food

Healthy nutrition is important to growth and development. Give your children opportunities to make choices from a variety of nutritious foods.

o "YOU NEED TO EAT VEGETABLES. WHICH DO YOU WANT TO EAT TODAY—PEAS OR CORN?"

o "YOU HAVE HAD ENOUGH CANDY FOR TODAY, BUT YOU MAY HAVE A SNACK. WOULD YOU LIKE CRACKERS AND CHEESE, OR AN APPLE?"

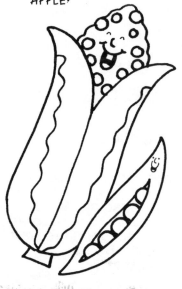

Chores

o GETTING CHILDREN TO CLEAN UP IS A CHORE IN AND OF ITSELF. GIVING OPTIONS HELPS TO MINIMIZE ARGUMENTS AND HASSLE. "WHEN DO YOU WANT TO PICK UP YOUR TOYS— BEFORE DINNER OR AFTER?" "YOU NEED TO CLEAN YOUR ROOM. WILL YOU DO IT TONIGHT OR TOMORROW MORNING?"

o MAKE A LIST OF CHORES. DECIDE WHO WILL DO WHAT CHORES AND WHEN THEY WILL BE DONE. GIVE EVERYONE A CHOICE, THEN WRITE TIMES AND NAMES AFTER THE CHORE. POST THE LIST IN A PROMINENT PLACE.

Adult Decisions

There are some situations or occasions that call for adults to make decisions because of safety or values. Be honest. Tell children that this is a time when an adult decision must be made. "I am older and need to make this decision. This is one time that you cannot decide. It is not safe for you to do that." (Remember to give a reason for your action. This helps them to feel secure and helps build their self-esteem rather than feeling put down.)

Prayer

Dear Jesus, our lives are full of decisions. Help us to make them according to Your will and enable our children to do the same. Hear our prayer, Oh Lord. Amen.

CONSEQUENCES OF OUR ACTIONS

by Marti Beuschlein

A man reaps what he sows (Galatians 6:7).

"Don't touch the pan on the stove. It is hot and you will burn yourself." How many times have we told our children this? As adults, we know how dangerous many things are that children attempt, but young children do not. Understanding the connection between their behavior and the consequences of that behavior is learned. We are the ones who can help them make the connection.

Natural Consequences

Natural consequences occur as a direct result of a specific behavior. They provide some of the best learning opportunities children can have. It is essential, however, that we protect children from actions that result in natural consequences that would be dangerous or harmful. "You ran too fast without looking where you were going and hurt your knee."

Social Consequences

Social consequences are the reactions of others to behavior. Children need to realize that their actions affect others. "That hurts Katie when you pinch her." "Ask Jared for the toy. People don't like grabbing." "It hurts your sister when you call her stupid."

Expectations and Consequences

Make children aware of your expectations and the consequences of not fulfilling them. State your expectations using simple and clear language so that children can understand. Often children misbehave because they are not fully aware of what is expected from them.

- "WE ARE GOING TO CHURCH. THERE WILL BE A LOT OF PEOPLE WHO WANT TO WORSHIP GOD AND HEAR THE PASTOR. WE NEED TO LISTEN AND NOT TALK WHILE THE PASTOR IS TALKING. WE CAN SING AND TALK WHEN IT IS OUR TURN."

- "WE ARE GOING TO NANA'S HOUSE AND SHE HAS A LOT OF BEAUTIFUL THINGS SITTING AROUND. YOU WILL NEED TO BE VERY CAREFUL AND REMEMBER NOT TO TOUCH ANYTHING. TELL HER HOW LOVELY HER THINGS ARE AND SHE MIGHT TELL YOU ABOUT THEM."

Making Unwise Decisions Cause Consequences

Allow children to experience the logical consequences of their behavior. They need to discover for themselves that unwise decisions may bring unpleasant results. "I'm sorry Nathan; I know that you want that book, but you spent your money on candy. It was your choice to make."

Prayer

Dear Lord, keep my children safe from the harm and danger that the consequences of their actions might bring to them. Give me wisdom to guide them according to Your will. Forgive me for the times I fail and lead me to share the gift of Your forgiveness with my children.
Amen.

Consequences That Might Happen

Children need to become more aware of the behaviors of others. Discuss things you might see during a television show or as you ride in the car. Help the children to think about the consequences of these behaviors. Talk about actions that are God-pleasing. "Is that a way to show God's love to others?" "Should that man have done that? What would you have done." "What is a better way to do that?"

PROBLEM SOLVING

by Marti Beuschlein

He will call upon me, and I will answer Him; I will be with Him in trouble, I will deliver Him and honor Him. (Psalm 91:15)

Children need Christ-centered foundations and roots so that they might become independent adults serving their Lord and Savior Jesus Christ. Part of the progress in our children's life journey is learning to solve their own problems in a God-pleasing manner. As parents, we need to begin this process when our children are very young.

How Do You Help Your Child Solve Problems?

o **IDENTIFY THE PROBLEM.** POINTING OUT SMALL SOLUTIONS IS A GOOD BEGINNING TO PROBLEM SOLVING. "UH-OH, IT LOOKS LIKE THAT SHOE WON'T FIT ON THAT FOOT." LEARNING TO IDENTIFY SMALL PROBLEMS LIKE THESE HELP PREPARE CHILDREN FOR BIGGER ONES AS WELL. "IT BOTHERS YOU WHEN EDDIE HITS YOU IN SCHOOL."

o **LISTEN.** LISTEN WITH YOUR EYES AND YOUR EARS. MAINTAIN EYE CONTACT AND LISTEN TO WHAT YOUR CHILDREN HAVE TO SAY ABOUT THEIR PROBLEMS.

o **BRAINSTORM POSSIBLE SOLUTIONS.** "HOW CAN WE MAKE THE SHOES FIT THE CORRECT FEET?" "LET'S TALK ABOUT WHAT YOU COULD DO WHEN EDDIE HITS YOU." "WHAT ELSE COULD YOU DO?" "IS THERE ANOTHER WAY TO DO THAT?" HELP YOUR CHILDREN COME UP WITH ONE OR MORE SOLUTIONS.

o **CHOOSE A SOLUTION AND TRY IT OUT.** "LET'S SEE IF THIS WORKS."

o **EVALUATE THE SOLUTION.** "HOW DO YOU THINK THAT WORKED?"

o **ENCOURAGE YOUR CHILDREN AS THEY SOLVE PROBLEMS.** "YOU'RE DOING A GOOD JOB PUTTING THOSE SHOES ON THE CORRECT FEET." "WOW! IT LOOKS LIKE YOU FEEL GOOD WHEN YOU AND EDDIE AREN'T FIGHTING."

o **PRAY TOGETHER FOR GOD'S HELP IN CHOOSING THE CORRECT SOLUTION TO A PROBLEM.**

Hints

o HELP YOUR CHILDREN LEARN THAT FORGIVENESS IS PART OF PROBLEM SOLVING.

o WHEN YOU ENCOUNTER BEHAVIOR PROBLEMS WITH YOUR CHILDREN, TRY SOLVING THEM TOGETHER INSTEAD OF SCOLDING. "I HAVE A PROBLEM. IT WORRIES ME WHEN YOU WANDER AWAY FROM ME IN THE STORE. WHAT CAN YOU DO DIFFERENTLY?"

o SEARCH FOR MORE INFORMATION AS NEEDED FOR PROBLEM SOLVING. "LET'S GO TO THE LIBRARY AND LOOK FOR A BOOK THAT WILL TELL US MORE ABOUT THAT."

o REMEMBER THAT NOT ALL SOLUTIONS YOUR CHILDREN COME UP WITH WILL BE ACCEPTABLE TO YOU OR APPROPRIATE FOR THE SITUATION. SUGGEST OTHER OPTIONS AND CHOICES THEY MIGHT MAKE.

o BE OPEN AND HONEST. SOME PROBLEMS CANNOT BE SOLVED THEIR WAY OR CANNOT BE SOLVED AT ALL. CHILDREN NEED TO KNOW THIS ALSO. IT'S PART OF GROWING AND LEARNING.

o WORK ON PROBLEMS ACCORDING TO THE INTEREST LEVEL OF YOUR CHILDREN. DON'T TRY TO GET THEM TO SOLVE A PROBLEM THAT THEY ARE NOT INTERESTED IN. IT IS ONLY DEFEATING FOR THEM.

Every person who works and lives with young children knows that it is impossible to sit down and problem-solve every situation with them. Seize those precious moments, times, and opportunities that naturally happen. It's worth the extra effort in the long run.

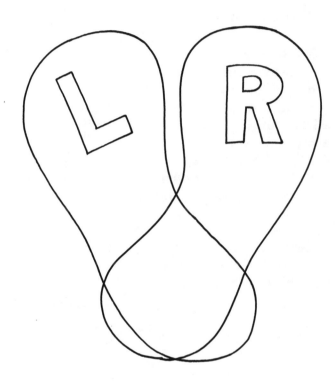

Prayer

Dear Father, give me wisdom to know how to encourage my children to solve their problems with Your blessing. Forgive me for the mistakes I make and help me to forgive my children for Jesus' sake. Amen.

Chapter Three
SPECIAL TIMES

Chapter Three
SPECIAL TIMES

Take That Baby Back

by Marti Beuschlein

Sons [and daughters] are a heritage from the LORD, children a reward from Him. (Psalm 127:3)

When Nathan visited his new brother in the hospital, he told his mommy and daddy to put the baby in the drawer next to the bed and close it ... tight! Three-year-old Nathan was, in no uncertain terms, unhappy about a new baby coming to his house to share his space and his parents.

Newborns, as cute and welcome as they are, can cause much stress. Parents are often sleep-deprived, tired, and trying to adjust to a change in their daily routine. Add siblings who are not quite sure of their new roles as big brothers or sisters, and you have a stressful family situation.

Parents can help create a happy and joyful celebration by including the siblings before and after the birth of a new baby.

Before the Birth

o PRAY TOGETHER, THANKING GOD FOR CREATING YOUR CHILDREN AND GIVING THE FAMILY A NEW BABY TO LOVE.

o BRING OUT BABY PICTURES AND MEMENTOS OF THE SIBLINGS' BIRTHS. TALK ABOUT HOW HAPPY YOU WERE WHEN GOD GAVE YOUR FAMILY A NEW BABY TO LOVE.

o IF POSSIBLE, VISIT A FRIEND WHO HAS AN INFANT OR SMALL CHILD. SHOW YOUR CHILDREN HOW MUCH CARE A BABY REQUIRES—SUCH AS FEEDING AND CHANGING DIAPERS.

o READ BOOKS ABOUT THE ARRIVAL OF A NEW MEMBER OF THE FAMILY. VISIT YOUR LOCAL LIBRARY OR ASK YOUR CHILDREN'S TEACHERS FOR SOME OF THE MANY BOOKS ABOUT NEW BABIES THAT ARE AVAILABLE.

o TALK ABOUT THINGS THEY CAN DO WHEN THEIR SIBLING ARRIVES. CAN THEY STACK THE DIAPERS OR CARRY DIRTY CLOTHES TO THE LAUNDRY ROOM? GIVE THEM SOME SPECIFIC RESPONSIBILITIES FROM WHICH THEY CAN CHOOSE. THIS WILL HELP THEM FEEL INVOLVED IN CARING FOR THE BABY INSTEAD OF JUST BEING AN ONLOOKER.

o ANSWER QUESTIONS YOUR CHILDREN MAY ASK ABOUT THE BIRTH. DON'T VOLUNTEER ANY MORE INFORMATION THAN THEY DESIRE. REMIND THEM THAT CHILDREN ARE A GIFT FROM GOD, GIVEN TO FAMILIES TO LOVE.

After the Birth

o WHILE IN THE HOSPITAL, SEND PACKETS OF SUGAR OR NAPKINS FROM YOUR MEAL TRAY TO YOUR CHILDREN AT HOME.

o PHOTOGRAPH OR VIDEO-TAPE THE FIRST MEETING OF BABY AND SIBLINGS, WHETHER AT HOME OR AT THE HOSPITAL.

o GIVE YOUR CHILDREN SPECIAL GIFTS (PACKED IN YOUR SUITCASE) TO CELEBRATE THEIR NEW ROLES AS BIG SISTERS OR BROTHERS .

o WHEN YOU ARRIVE HOME, HAVE DAD OR SOMEONE ELSE CARRY THE NEW BABY SO THAT YOU HAVE OPEN ARMS FOR THE OLDER CHILDREN.

o MAINTAIN YOUR CHILDREN'S DAILY ROUTINE AS MUCH AS POSSIBLE, KEEPING CHANGES IN THEIR SCHED-ULE MINIMAL. TRY TO KEEP THEIR BATH TIME, PLAYTIME, AND BEDTIME ROUTINES THE SAME AS BEFORE THE NEW BABY.

o WHILE BABY IS SLEEPING, SPEND SOME SPECIAL ONE-ON-ONE TIME WITH YOUR OTHER CHILDREN. SOMETIMES JUST LISTEN-ING TO YOUR CHILDREN IS ALL THAT IS NEEDED.

o GIVE YOUR CHILDREN A PIC-TURE OF THE NEW BABY TO TAKE TO SCHOOL. SEND A SPECIAL TREAT WITH YOUR CHILDREN TO SHARE WITH THEIR CLASSMATES.

o GIVE YOUR CHILDREN OPPORTUNITIES TO HELP IN THE CARE OF THE BABY.

o SAY THIS FINGER PLAY WITH YOUR CHILDREN.

Here is mommy.
(Point to index finger.)
Here is daddy.
(Point to middle finger.)
Here is
(insert your child's name) tall.
(Point to ring finger.)
Here is
baby (insert baby's name) small.
(Point to small finger.)
God loves us all!

(Hold up all fingers and wiggle them.)

To Remember

Children will react to the new baby no matter how well you prepare them. Their behavior can change in several different ways. They may resort to "baby" behavior, such as sucking their thumb, bathroom accidents, or "baby talk." Temper tantrums, shy-ness, or even asking you to "take the baby back" are other types of behavior that might occur.

Accept these changes in behavior with an extra measure of love and affection. They are often temporary and disappear as the family settles into their new pattern of family life.

Prayer

Heavenly Father, thank You for the gift of children. Empower us with Your Holy Spirit to live together as a family, loving and serving You, and each other. Forgive our sins and strengthen us with Your grace. In Jesus' name. Amen.

WHY IS THE MOVING VAN IN FRONT OF OUR HOUSE?

by Marti Beuschlein

"The LORD replied, "My Presence will go with you, and I will give you rest." (Exodus 33:14)

Three-year-old Jonathan was excited as he watched the movers unload the furniture into his new home. "There's my bed and our good ol' couch." He had honestly thought that his family's belongings had totally disappeared. Moving is often as difficult and stressful for young children as it is for adults.

Include the children

o AS YOU MAKE PLANS TO MOVE, INCLUDE YOUR CHILDREN IN THE PROCESS. TELL THEM WHY YOU ARE MOVING. "DADDY HAS A NEW JOB IN ANOTHER CITY AND WE NEED TO MOVE NEAR HIS JOB."

o KEEP A POSITIVE ATTITUDE ABOUT THE MOVE. CHILDREN SENSE NEGATIVE VIBES AND ATTITUDES. MAKE THE MOVE AN EXCITING AND NEW ADVENTURE.

o GIVE YOUR CHILDREN OPPORTUNITIES TO SOLVE PROBLEMS DURING THE MOVE. "WHICH TOYS DO YOU WANT TO TAKE ALONG WITH YOU AND WHICH ONES DO YOU WANT TO HAVE THE MOVERS TAKE?"

o PRAY TOGETHER ASKING GOD'S GUIDANCE AND PROTECTION FOR YOUR FAMILY MOVE.

o HAVE A FAMILY MEETING AND MAKE A LIST OF THINGS TO DO. LET THE CHILDREN CHOOSE AGE-APPROPRIATE TASKS THEY CAN DO TO HELP.

o INCLUDE THE CHILDREN AS MUCH AS POSSIBLE IN THE PACKING PROCESS.

Saying Good-bye

Saying good-bye to friends and neighbors is important. Have your children give pictures of themselves to friends, along with their new address.
Invite your children's friends to a picnic (in a park or your backyard) before the move for a memorable farewell together. Collect addresses so that your children can send pictures of their new home to their friends.

Pray together ...

Dear God, go with us to our new home. Keep us safe during our journey. Help us to treasure old friendships and to build new ones—always thanking You that Jesus, our Savior and Friend, is by our side. For Jesus' sake. Amen.

The New House

o IF A TRIP TO YOUR NEW HOME IS NOT POSSIBLE, SHOW A VIDEO OR PICTURES OF THE NEW HOUSE SO THAT YOUR CHILDREN CAN BECOME FAMILIAR WITH IT.

Together as a Family

Melody: "Here We Go 'Round the Mulberry Bush"

We are moving to a new home,
A new home, a new home.
God is going with us—
We are not alone.
We are making new friends,
New friends, new friends.
God is going with us—
We are not alone.

Prayer

Lord God, Giver of all good gifts, we thank You for the gift of a new home. Come into our home with Your presence and blessing. Make this a place of love, forgiveness, joy, happiness, and peace. In the name of Jesus we pray. Amen.

WAITING FOR BABY JESUS

by Marti Beuschlein

While they were there, the time came for the baby to be born, and she gave birth to her firstborn, a son. (Luke 2:6–7a)

The Countdown

An Advent calendar is an excellent way to help your children count the days until Jesus' birthday. Stop and take the time each day to open a door on the calendar. Do it with a special ceremony, devotion, or prayer.

I like preparing for Christmas—especially decorating and shopping for gifts. For Christians, preparing for Christmas takes on a different meaning than that of the secular world. We call this time Advent—a time to get ready to celebrate the coming of Jesus.

Waiting is difficult for young children and the season of Advent often gets hectic with shopping, baking, and decorating homes.

Make an effort to slow the pace and give your children the gift of time this Advent season—the time to get ready for Baby Jesus' birthday—and thus keep the true meaning of Christmas in focus.

Advent Togetherness

o INVOLVE YOUR CHILDREN IN CHRISTMAS PREPARATIONS.

o BAKE COOKIES TOGETHER. YOU WILL TREASURE THE MEMORIES YOU ARE MAKING.

o LET YOUR CHILDREN WRAP THE GIFTS THEY ARE GIVING. WHO WOULDN'T LOVE TO GET A GIFT WRAPPED BY A THREE-YEAR-OLD?

o TOGETHER MAKE A LIST OF "THINGS TO BE DONE BEFORE CHRISTMAS." GIVE YOUR CHILDREN CHOICES OF CHORES TO DO. EVEN YOUNG CHILDREN CAN HELP CLEAN AND DO EXTRA CHORES.

o INSTEAD OF SETTING OUT AN ENTIRE NATIVITY SET AT ONE TIME, BRING ONE PIECE OUT EACH DAY AND TALK ABOUT ITS PLACE IN THE CHRISTMAS STORY. "THIS IS MARY. MARY WAS JESUS' MOTHER." BABY JESUS WOULD BE THE LAST PIECE—HOPEFULLY ON CHRISTMAS EVE.

o GIVE YOUR CHILDREN A CORNER IN THE HOUSE OR THEIR ROOMS TO DECORATE. THE CHRISTMAS TREE IN OUR FAMILY ROOM WAS THE TREE THAT MY FOUR BOYS DECORATED WITH POPCORN, CRANBERRIES, AND PAPER CHAINS. I SAVED ALL OF THE ORNAMENTS THEY HAD MADE IN SCHOOL AND ADDED THEM TO "THEIR TREE." I STILL DECORATE THAT TREE WITH "THEIR" DECORATIONS.

Rest— Less Stress

This time of year can be very stressful. If at all possible, keep your stress level low and make sure that you and your children get enough rest.

Sit quietly and enjoy a hot cup of chocolate together. Enjoy looking at the beautiful tree that you have decorated together. Help your children to have warm, joyful memories.

Gifts

Arrange gifts under the tree according to the giver rather than the receiver. This will emphasize the giving of gifts. It helps your children focus on the gifts they are giving. Remind your children that we give gifts because God sent Baby Jesus and He is the best gift of all.

New Words to Learn

Help your child become acquainted with the vocabulary of the Christmas season and the story of Jesus' birth. Include a new word in each daily devotion during Advent.

Make a Christmas scrapbook by cutting and pasting magazine pictures onto brightly colored construction paper. Tie the pages together with a pretty ribbon.

Prayer

Come, Lord Jesus, especially as we prepare to celebrate Your coming into our world as Savior. Come, Lord Jesus, with Your blessings of love, forgiveness, peace, and joy. Amen.

GRANDPA DIED

by Marti Beuschlein

[Jesus said,] "I am the resurrection and the life. He who believes in Me will live, even though he dies; and whoever lives and believes in Me will never die." (John 11:25)

Our preschool playground was located right next to the church's cemetery. There was no fence, and children often wandered into the cemetery. One day a little girl shouted, "I think one of them is trying to get out. Come quick." Of course the whole class ran over—including me, the teacher. Lori had found a crack in the dry ground near a tombstone and figured that someone was escaping. Thus began a lesson about death.

There is no easy way to talk about death with young children. Death is an abstract concept and children think in concrete terms—what they can see is what they understand. What happens after death cannot be seen, therefore it is difficult to understand.

children's Views on Death

o **INFANTS/TODDLERS** WILL SENSE THE EMOTIONS AND FEELINGS OF ADULTS AND REACT TO THEM.

o **THREE- TO FIVE-YEAR-OLDS** WILL BE CURIOUS ABOUT DEATH BUT MAY THINK OF DEATH AS REVERSIBLE. THEY DO NOT CLEARLY UNDERSTAND THE FINALITY OF DEATH.

o **SIX- TO NINE-YEAR-OLDS** WILL DEVELOP A CLEARER UNDERSTANDING OF DEATH, SENSING THAT IT IS FINAL. THEY REALIZE THAT THEY TOO CAN DIE AND BEGIN TO FEAR DEATH.

o **TEN-YEARS-OLD AND OLDER** WILL BE MORE READY TO FACE THE LOGICAL ASPECTS OF DEATH AND ITS BIOLOGICAL RESULTS.

o **TEENAGERS** OFTEN THINK THAT SINCE THEY ARE YOUNG, DEATH IS IN THE DISTANT FUTURE.

It is crucial that adults understand their own private and personal perspective of death before they can help young children. Talk with your pastor about your own concerns and questions. Ask God for His guidance and assurance.

Handling Death with Children

- GIVE SIMPLE, DIRECT ANSWERS TO CHILDREN'S QUESTIONS ABOUT DEATH.

- DO NOT COMPARE DEATH WITH SLEEP OR GOING AWAY. CHILDREN MAY THINK THE PERSON WHO HAS DIED WILL WAKE UP OR COME BACK. AVOID SAYING THAT SOMEONE DIED BECAUSE THEY WERE SICK (CHILDREN MAY THINK IF THEY BECOME SICK THEY WILL ALSO DIE).

"GRANDPA DIED AND WENT TO HEAVEN TO LIVE WITH JESUS. WE WILL NOT SEE HIM ANYMORE HERE ON EARTH, SOMEDAY WE WILL ALL BE TOGETHER IN HEAVEN"

- KEEP DAILY ROUTINES AS NORMAL AS POSSIBLE. MAKE SURE YOUR CHILDREN ARE SURROUNDED WITH FAMILIAR PEOPLE AND OBJECTS SO THEY CAN FEEL SAFE AND SECURE.

- INCLUDE CHILDREN IN THE GRIEVING PROCESS. ATTENDING THE FUNERAL WITH LOVING AND CARING FAMILY MEMBERS HELPS BRING CLOSURE FOR CHILDREN. ACCEPT THEIR FEELINGS AND SUPPORT THEM IN THEIR SORROW.

- READ AGE-APPROPRIATE BOOKS ABOUT DEATH AND DYING TO YOUR CHILDREN. ASK YOUR PASTORS, TEACHERS, OR LIBRARIAN FOR SUGGESTIONS.

- LISTEN FOR CLUES TELLING YOU HOW MUCH AND WHEN TO TALK ABOUT DEATH.

Prayer

O Living Lord, the idea of death is frightening for both adults and children. Help us to minister to each other as we mourn. Fill us with Your peace and help us to live in hope because of Your resurrection and love. As You promised, wipe away our tears. Amen.

When a Pet Dies

A child's first experience with death is always difficult. Deal with it in an honest and truthful way. Don't cover up the death, (i.e. getting a new pet and passing it off as the pet that has died.) The death of a pet can open doors for a discussion about death. Accept their grief over a pet's death.

HOLIDAYS, CELEBRATIONS, & CHILDREN

by Marti Beuschlein

Then all the people went away to eat and drink, to send portions of food and to celebrate with great joy, because they now understood the words that had been made known to them. (Nehemiah 8:12)

For young children, holidays can be both a joy and a disaster waiting to happen. The same can be true for adults. Perhaps these suggestions can help make your celebrations and holidays more joyful and happy for everyone.

Holiday Hints

○ TALK ABOUT TREASURED MEMORIES AS YOU BUILD FAMILY TRADITIONS. "WHEN I WAS ABOUT YOUR AGE WE ATE A BIG THANKSGIVING DINNER AT MY GRANDMOTHER'S HOUSE." BUILD ON OLD TRADITIONS AND CREATE NEW ONES YOUR FAMILY CAN ENJOY TOGETHER.

○ MAKE EACH PERSON'S BIRTHDAY A UNIQUE EVENT. ONE FAMILY I KNOW HAS A SPECIAL BIRTHDAY PLATE USED BY THE BIRTHDAY PERSON. IN OUR FAMILY, THE BIRTHDAY PERSON COULD ASK FOR ANYTHING THEY WANTED FOR DINNER.

○ EVERY YEAR, OUR FAMILY HAD AN EASTER BASKET HUNT AS WE LOOKED FOR HIDDEN BASKETS HOLDING INEXPENSIVE ITEMS SUCH AS A NEW HAIRBRUSH OR FAVORITE HOMEMADE FOOD. THE TRADITION CONTINUED UNTIL MY FOUR SONS LEFT TO ESTABLISH THEIR OWN HOMES, TAKING THEIR BASKETS WITH THEM. ONE DAUGHTER-IN-LAW USES IT AS PART OF THEIR HOME DECORATIONS, WHILE ANOTHER PASSED THE BASKET ON TO THEIR SON AS HIS EASTER BASKET.)

○ FIND WAYS TO HELP SHIFT YOUR CHILDREN'S THINKING FROM RECEIVING GIFTS TO SHARING WITH OTHERS. TOGETHER, BAKE A SPECIAL TREAT FOR A HOMEBOUND NEIGHBOR OR MEMBER OF YOUR CONGREGATION. INCLUDE YOUR CHILDREN IN PACKAGING OR DISTRIBUTING FOOD THROUGH A CHURCH OR COMMUNITY PROJECT.

Remember, happy holidays are made of warm loving families creating family traditions and enjoying each other.

More Is Not Always Better

Parties and gifts do not have to be expensive and elaborate. Children enjoy simple things, so make their parties simple and fun.

My grown sons' holiday memories are of family traditions that were inexpensive, but required a lot of family togetherness. Interestingly enough, they are passing down these same traditions as they raise their own children.

Prayer

Thank You, Lord Jesus, for the happy times in our lives—for holy days and parties, celebrations, and family traditions. Bless our use of all these good times to thank You for Your grace and to teach our children the joy of faith. Thank You, Jesus. We love You. Amen.

FAMILY FUN

Chips

Are We There Yet?

by Marti Beuschlein

"O Lord you will keep us safe and protect us." (Psalm 12:7)

Hints for Happy Travel Time

o HELP EACH CHILD FIND A "PERSONAL SPACE." EVERYONE STAYS IN THEIR PERSONAL SPACE UNLESS INVITED INTO ANOTHER BY THE OWNER.

o A TRAVEL BAG FOR EACH OF THE CHILDREN IS A MUST. GIVE THEM THE CHOICE OF ITEMS TO PUT INTO THE BAG. ALL PERSONAL ITEMS THEY WANT TO TAKE ON THE TRIP NEED TO FIT INTO THIS BAG.

o TAKE ALONG A PILLOW AND SMALL BLANKET FOR EACH CHILD.

o PURCHASE SMALL SURPRISE GIFTS TO BE GIVEN DAILY. ON THE FIRST DAY GIVE A NOTEBOOK TO BE USED AS A JOURNAL. THOSE WHO CANNOT WRITE CAN DRAW PICTURES. OTHER GIFTS CAN BE SNACKS, A NEW BOX OF CRAYONS, OR SILLY ITEMS THAT WILL MAKE THEM LAUGH.

o OLDER READERS CAN BE "TOURIST GUIDE" FOR THE DAY. HAVE THEM READ AHEAD IN A GUIDEBOOK OR MAP, THEN TELL THE HISTORY OR INTERESTING FACTS ABOUT EACH PLACE. FIND OUT THE STATE FLOWER, TREE, AND FLAG FOR EACH STATE VISITED.

o TAKE CASSETTE TAPES WITH SING-ALONG SONGS AND DO SOME FAMILY SINGING. LISTEN TO DEVOTIONAL TAPES. ASK YOUR TEACHER FOR SUGGESTIONS.

My pastor husband and I had not taken a vacation for five years.

Our congregation gave us a vacation as a gift. We hooked up our pop-top camper trailer to our station wagon and loaded four boys—4, 5 ½, 8 and 10—and a variety of baggage. Then we left Chicago and headed to California for a six-week journey. And what a jouney it was!

The boys in the back seat built a "great conflict wall" of picnic baskets, Styrofoam containers, and anything else they could find.

We made an "emergency" stop at the nearest discount store where I purchased four large canvas bags and lots of items that would keep the interest of four boys.

It turned out to be the best family vacation we ever had. Our boys tell stories to their own children about our famous six-week trip to California, and have many fond memories of it.

That's what family vacations are all about—building memories, enjoying each other, spending time together, seeing new things in God's world, and having fun!

- Involve the children in planning the vacation.

- Buy postcards from the places you visit or make stops. Play games in the car using the postcards. Pick a postcard and tell your favorite thing about that place. Make up a story about the postcard. Tell everything you remember about that particular place.

- Have a short devotion each day before beginning your journey. Everyone in the family can take turns leading the devotions. Use the form below as a guideline for your devotions.

Travel Devotion

Bible Reading:
Take turns reading a Bible verse or a portion of Scripture. Younger children can say Bible words or tell Bible stories that they know from memory.

Song:
Sing a favorite song about God and His love.

God Is with Us (Melody: "Are You Sleeping?")

God is with us, God is with us
As we travel, as we travel.
He is always with us.
He is always watching.
God is here. God loves us.
Make up new verses.

Prayer:

Vary the prayer each day. Use "echo style" prayers (leader says a line and others repeat the same line), circle prayers, or response prayers (leader prays and others say a three or four word response).
Dear Lord, be with us today as we travel. Keep us safe. Help us to love one another like You love us. We praise and worship You. In Your name we pray. Amen.

Summer Time Fun

by Marti Beuschlein

"Let us rejoice and be glad and give Him glory."
(Revelation 19:7)

Summer time is a good time to renew family life. There are many opportunities to spend more time together. Celebrate and explore God's world. Create memories. Appreciate the gifts God has given to each of you. Learn something new and grow together in Christ.

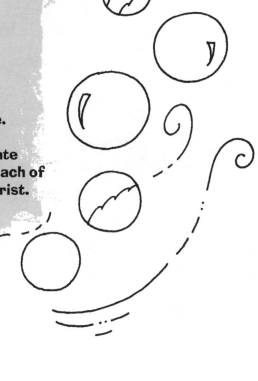

Sensational Sun Fun

o MARK A FIVE-FOOT SQUARE IN YOUR BACK YARD WITH STRING OR TAPE. USE A MAGNIFYING GLASS TO SEE HOW MANY THINGS YOU CAN FIND IN THAT SPACE. MAKE A LIST OF THE ITEMS.

o MAKE A WIND CHIME. CHOOSE A BRANCH OR PIECE OF DRIFT WOOD TO USE AS A BASE FOR THE WIND CHIME. DRILL HOLES IN THE BRANCH OR WOOD. FIND OLD METAL ITEMS AROUND THE HOUSE SUCH AS KITCHEN UTENSILS, TOOLS, OR TIN CANS. TIE THEM TO THE BASE WITH STRING OR FISHING LINE. MAKE SURE THEY HANG CLOSE ENOUGH TOGETHER TO MAKE A NOISE.

o INVITE FRIENDS OF YOUR CHILDREN AND THEIR FAMILIES ON A PICNIC. HAVE THE PICNIC AT A NEARBY PARK OR IN YOUR BACK YARD. INVOLVE YOUR CHILDREN IN PLANNING THE PICNIC.

o HAVE A FAMILY WATER FIGHT ON A HOT SUMMER DAY.

o LIE DOWN AND LOOK AT THE CLOUDS. FIND DIFFERENT SHAPES AND FORMS. GO TO THE LIBRARY AND GET A BOOK ABOUT CLOUDS. LEARN THE NAMES OF EACH VARIETY.

o VISIT AN HISTORIC SITE. COLLECT BROCHURES AND TAKE PICTURES. WRITE A STORY ABOUT YOUR VISIT. PUT THE STORY, PICTURES, AND BROCHURES IN A SCRAPBOOK.

o DECLARE A "FUN AND WASH" DAY — WASH THE CAR, BICYCLES, OUTDOOR FURNITURE, OR PETS. THANK GOD FOR WATER AND FUN.

o PUT SEVERAL OBJECTS SUCH AS A SPOON, A SPOOL OF THREAD, AND A CROSS ON A DARK PIECE OF PAPER. PLACE IN DIRECT SUNLIGHT FOR SEVERAL HOURS. BRING INDOORS AND SEE THE PATTERNS THE SUN HAS MADE. USE THE PAPER AS A CENTERPIECE FOR THE DINNER TABLE.

o HAVE A FAMILY CAMPOUT IN THE BACK YARD. PITCH A TENT OR SLEEP IN SLEEPING BAGS UNDER THE STARS. MAKE A CAMPFIRE IN THE CHARCOAL GRILL. ROAST MARSHMALLOWS AND TELL STORIES.

- LIE ON YOUR BACKS AND LOOK AT THE STARS. CHECK OUT LIBRARY BOOKS AND LEARN ABOUT THE STAR CONSTELLATIONS. TRY TO COUNT THE STARS. READ THE STORY OF ABRAHAM AND THE STARS (GENESIS 22:17). THANK GOD FOR STARS AND THE MANY BLESSINGS HE GIVES YOU.

- TAKE A DRIVE TO THE COUNTRY. STOP AT A FARM STAND. TALK TO THE FARMER ABOUT HOW VEGETABLES ARE GROWN. BUY SOME FRESH VEGETABLES.

- BUY A POTATO OR CARROT. CUT OFF THE TOP AND INSERT TOOTHPICKS ON EITHER SIDE OF THE VEGGIE. PLACE THE TOOTHPICKS ON THE RIM OF A GLASS FILLED WITH WATER SO THAT THE BOTTOM OF THE VEGETABLE SITS IN THE WATER. WATCH ROOTS FORM AND SPROUTS GROW FROM THE TOP.

Prayer

**Heavenly Father,
I thank You for celebrations,
summer time, and my family.
You have given us
so many good gifts.
Teach us to appreciate them
and use them to Your glory.
Thank You for Your love and
care through Jesus.
We praise and worship You.
Amen.**

TAKE A HIKE

by Marti Beuschlein

"This is what the LORD says: Stand at the crossroads and look; ask for the ancient paths, ask where the good way is, and walk in it, and you will find rest for your souls."
(Jeremiah 6:16)

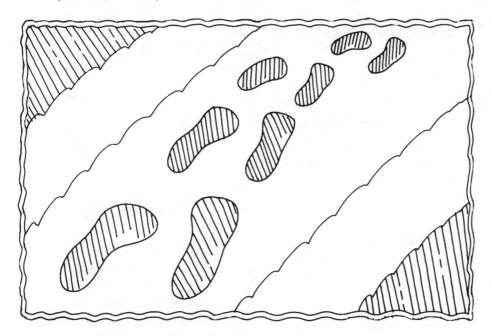

Neighborhood Walk

Following are suggestions for different kinds of walks you can take with your children.

After each walk, share the experience using the discussion ideas. Encourage your children to draw pictures of your walk together and to tell you about the picture. Write the story as dictated on the back of the picture.

Keep a "walking bag" near your door. Fill the bag with items that you might use on a walk, such as ...

- Bottled water

- Camera

- Binoculars

- Plastic bags to hold found treasures

- Sunscreen

- A small first aid kit

Walk around the block and look at the different houses. Talk about how the houses are different and alike. Try to guess what people are doing inside. Are they eating dinner? Watching TV?

Discussion: God made everyone special and different. We are not all alike. Some people have dogs; others have cats. Some plant flowers in their yard; some plant trees. We are different, but one thing is the same: God loves us all and He sent Jesus to be our Savior.

Rainy Day Walk

Take a walk on a sprinkly, rainy day. Observe how different the trees, flowers, and street look in the rain. Feel the raindrops, the shrubs, and grass. And yes, splash in a puddle—just wear good rainwear.

Discussion: God gives us rain to help plants grow and to wash away the dirt on plants and houses. God also washes away all the wrong that we do through the waters of Baptism and through Jesus. He forgives our sins and promises eternal life.

Snowy Day Walk

If you live in an area where it snows, take a walk. Listen to the quiet. Make footprints in the snow. Look for other footprints—animal and human. How are they different? Are the footprints bigger or smaller than yours? ? Make angels in the snow.

Discussion: God gives us snow. Thank God for the beautiful snow and the opportunity to enjoy His wonderful world.

Treasure Hunt Walk

Look for nature treasures you can pick up and put in a plastic bag (i.e., twigs, leaves, rocks, pine cones, etc.). When you arrive back home, help your child sort the treasures. Put the rough items in one pile, smooth in another. Find the shiny and dull objects.

Discussion: Thank God for giving us eyes to see His world and all the things He created.

Listening Walk

On this walk listen to the various sounds. Are there dogs barking? Birds singing? Do you hear TVs playing in the houses? What does wind sound like? You might want to take along a tape recorder to record the various sounds you hear. When you return home, replay the sounds and have your child identify them.

Discussion: Thank God for giving us ears to hear different sounds in His world.

Walk Safely

Remember to be safe while taking a hike. Remind your child to always stay near you. Hold hands for safety and for closeness. Put on sunscreen if needed.

Prayer

Dear Lord, thank You for placing us in a wonderful world that is full of reminders that You are great and glorious. Help us to stay focused on You and Your love as we walk through Your world each day. Amen.

Chapter Five

AT SCHOOL

SCHOOL DAYS—A NEW BEGINNING

by Marti Beuschlein

Train a child in the way he should go, and when he is old he will not turn from it. (Proverbs 22:6)

Walking into a new environment can be intimidating and downright frightening. Even returning to a familiar classroom after a long summer or holiday break can be intimidating. Your children may experience many different emotions ranging from joy and excitement to feeling nervous, lonely, and lost. In addition, your children are often caught between their need to be near you and to be out on their own.

Getting Ready for School

o READ BOOKS THAT FEATURE "FIRST DAY AT SCHOOL" THEMES. DRAW A CORRELATION BETWEEN THE EXPERIENCES IN THE BOOK TO THOSE OF YOUR CHILDREN. GIVE THEM AN OPPORTUNITY TO TALK ABOUT THEIR FEELINGS OR ASK QUESTIONS ABOUT WHAT TO EXPECT AT THEIR NEW SCHOOL.

o VISIT THE CLASSROOMS WITH YOUR CHILDREN BEFORE THE FIRST DAY OF SCHOOL TO BECOME ACQUAINTED WITH THE TEACHERS AND THEIR NEW ENVIRONMENT.

o IF AT ALL POSSIBLE, INVITE THE TEACHERS TO VISIT YOUR HOME. SEEING THE TEACHER IN THEIR HOME WILL HELP YOUR CHILDREN FEEL MORE SECURE.

o CREATE A "SPECIAL TIME" WITH YOUR CHILDREN BEFORE SCHOOL BEGINS. GO OUT FOR ICE CREAM THE NIGHT BEFORE OR HAVE A SPECIAL BREAKFAST THE FIRST MORNING OF SCHOOL.

o REMEMBER TO ASK GOD TO BE WITH YOUR CHILDREN IN YOUR REGULAR PRAYERS.

o TOGETHER SELECT THE CLOTHES TO WEAR THE FIRST DAY OF SCHOOL AND LAY THEM OUT IN YOUR CHILDREN'S ROOMS. SHARE YOUR RECOLLECTION OF YOUR FIRST DAY OF SCHOOL AS YOU PREPARE FOR THEIR FIRST DAY. TALK ABOUT SOME OF THE THINGS THEY WILL DO.

At School

- **Sing this song on the way to school.**

  Melody: "Mary Had a Little Lamb."

  I am going to school today,
  school today, school today.
  I am going to school today,
  And I will have some fun!

  Add different words
  such as:

  I am going to paint today ...
  I am going to sing today ...
  I am going to play today ...

- DEVELOP A GOOD-BYE RITUAL. DO NOT SLIP OUT WHEN YOUR CHILDREN ARE NOT LOOKING. DECIDE HOW MANY KISSES AND HUGS YOU WILL GIVE BEFORE LEAVING. TELL WHERE YOU WILL BE AND WHAT YOU WILL BE DOING. LET THEM KNOW YOU WILL BE BACK TO GET THEM. OPEN AND HONEST GOOD-BYES BUILD TRUST.

Happy Transitions

Use these suggestions if your children are having a difficult time making the transition between home and school.

- WRITE A NOTE TO PUT IN THEIR POCKETS THAT TELLS THEM THE TIME YOU WILL PICK THEM UP. LET THEM SEE YOU WRITE THE NOTE AND TELL THEM WHAT IT SAYS. IT'S A SMALL COMFORT AND REMINDER THAT YOU WILL COME FOR THEM.

- HELP YOUR CHILDREN CHOOSE AN ITEM THAT BELONGS TO YOU SUCH AS A SCARF, GLOVE, OR OLD WALLET. LET THEM TAKE IT TO SCHOOL AS A REMINDER THAT YOU WILL BE BACK TO GET THEM.

- ARRIVE EARLY THE FIRST FEW DAYS SO THAT YOU CAN STAY FOR AWHILE AND HELP YOUR CHILDREN GET INVOLVED IN FUN ACTIVITIES BEFORE YOU LEAVE.

- GIVE YOUR CHILDREN A FAMILY PICTURE TO LOOK AT IF THEY GET LONELY.

Family Devotion

Use this as a special family devotion the night before the first day of school:

Bible Words:

"I am with you always."
(Matthew 28:20)

Song:
Melody: "Are You Sleeping?"

God is with me. God is with me.
At my school. At my school.
God is always with me.
God is always with me.
He loves me. He loves me.

Prayer:

Dear Lord and Savior,
be with (insert names of
your children) as they go
to school tomorrow.

Keep them safe.
Help them to remember
that You are walking by
their side. Fill them with
peace and joy.
In Your name we pray.
Amen.

WHAT DID YOU DO IN SCHOOL TODAY?

by Marti Beuschlein

Listen, my son, to your father's instruction and do not forsake your mother's teaching. They will be a garland to grace your head and a chain to adorn your neck. (Proverbs 1:8)

As Carol picked up Kasey she asked, "What did you do in school today?" She was looking for an exciting recounting of his day's activities; instead she got the nonchalant reply of "Nothing!"

Young children cannot always recall an entire day's events, then give a running description at a moment's notice. They have been very busy the entire day. Since most children live in a "here and now" time-frame, the last activity in which they were engaged will be uppermost in their mind.

Sometimes children simply lack the words to describe their day. Try some of these ideas to help you and your children share your days with one another.

Helpful Language

○ BE SPECIFIC: "WHAT DID YOU HAVE FOR SNACK?" "TELL ME ABOUT YOUR (PAINTING, PICTURE, OR PROJECT)." "WHAT STORY DID YOUR TEACHER READ?" "WHO DID YOU PLAY WITH? WHAT DID YOU PLAY?"

○ ASK QUESTIONS THAT INVITE A MORE DETAILED RESPONSE THAN JUST ONE WORD.

Keep Informed

Keep informed by talking to teachers and reading newsletters and other information sent home. Check out parent bulletin boards.

Use this information to ask specific questions such as "Where did you go on your walk today?" "Tell me about the food that you cooked today. What was it called?"

Sharing Times

Perhaps "pick-up time" is not best for sharing the activities of the day. These might be better times and places:

o DURING AN AFTER-SCHOOL SNACK, SITTING AT THE KITCHEN TABLE

o DURING THE EVENING MEAL WHEN EVERYONE IS SHARING. GIVE THE YOUNGEST CHILDREN AN OPPORTUNITY TO SHARE THEIR DAY.

o WHILE SHOPPING FOR THE EVENING'S MEAL ON THE WAY HOME FROM SCHOOL

o IN THE CAR AS YOU SIT IN A TRAFFIC JAM OR WAIT AT A LONG RED LIGHT

o AT BATHTIME

o AT BEDTIME AS YOU TUCK THEM IN

o AT PRAYER TIME, INCORPORATING THE DAY'S ACTIVITIES INTO THE PRAYER

Sharing Song

Use this song to help your children recall the activities of their day. You sing the first verse naming something you did today. Then your child sings a verse. Continue taking turns sharing verses.

Melody: "Here We Go 'Round the Mulberry Bush"

Today in school I _____
(played with play dough, sang a song, painted a picture, etc.)
_____ (repeat), _____
(repeat).
Today in school I _____
(repeat),
I had so much fun!

Prayer

Gracious Father, give me patience for waiting until my children are ready to tell me about their day. Help me to give them the undivided attention they need and to share Your gracious love and forgiveness with them. In Jesus' name. Amen.

SEE WHAT I MADE

by Marti Beuschlein

"Let your light shine before men, that they may see your good deeds and praise your Father in heaven ..."
(Matthew 5:16)

God created young children to be creative. My son Peter was a habitual junk collector as a young child. He collected "stuff" that he found—in wastebaskets or on the street—or that found its way into his pocket or his room. Then he created *more junk* from his treasures.

My teacher training and my needs as a mother had many battles over Peter's creative adventures. Most often my teacher training won, and Peter created his little heart out. I'm thankful because today he is a very creative young man who can still find ways to make something out of nothing. And yes, he is still a junk collector!

Creative Art Enhances Learning

Art for children ...

o IS A GROWING EXPERIENCE.

o IS USING IMAGINATION VIA PURPLE GRASS, RED CLOUDS, TWO-HEADED DADDIES, AND BIG BLOBS OF BROWN PAINT.

o IS EXCITING—TRYING NEW COLORS, TEXTURES, SHAPES, SIZES, AND DIFFERENT MATERIALS.

o IS UNIQUE. NO TWO PIECES OF ARTWORK ARE THE SAME.

o HELPS CLARIFY AND UNDERSTAND GOD'S WORLD.

o HELPS DEVELOP INDEPENDENT THINKING.

o HELPS EXPRESS FEELINGS.

o IS A PART OF THEM. THEY HAVE PUT THEIR FEELINGS, EXPRESSIONS, AND IMPRESSIONS OF WHAT THEY SEE AND UNDERSTAND ON PAPER.

o IS FUN!

The point of this story is that adults need to give children opportunities to use the natural, creative ability God has given them. Too often we stifle creativity with our own rigid rules.

Our job is to provide the materials, space, time, and atmosphere for children to create unique and wonderful works of art they can call their very own.

It is also our job to value and appreciate the artwork done by our children—the colors, bold strokes, and delightful designs—instead of only evaluating the end result. After all, the process of creating is just as important as the final product.

Display These Works of Art

We show children that we value them and their works of art by displaying the artwork in prominent places—
on the refrigerator, on the back of a door, in the family room, down the hallway, or on a bulletin board.

o MAKE A SPECIAL SIGN FOR THE ART GALLERY TO IDENTIFY THE ARTIST.

o TAKE PICTURES OF THE CREATED WORKS TO DISPLAY IF THERE IS A LACK OF SPACE.

o FIND A PLACE TO STORE THE CREATIONS TO GIVE TO YOUR CHILDREN WHEN THEY GET MARRIED.
(I GAVE ALL OF PETER'S BEAUTIFUL JUNK TO HIS BRIDE IN A DECORATED BOX. SHE LOVES AND TREASURES IT.)

Children Learn through Art

Children grow in *physical/perceptual development*:

o FINE MOTOR CONTROL

o VISUAL AND SPATIAL AWARENESS

o EYE-HAND COORDINATION

o SHAPE, SIZE, AND COLOR DISCRIMINATION

o TACTILE/KINESTHETIC AWARENESS

Children grow in *cognitive development*:

o PROBLEM SOLVING

o UNDERSTANDING CAUSE AND EFFECT

o COMMUNICATING NONVERBAL IDEAS

o SEQUENCING EVENTS

Children grow in *social and emotional development*:

o AESTHETIC GROWTH

o COOPERATION AND SHARING—E.G., TAKING TURNS

o RESOLVE INTERPERSONAL CONFLICTS

o APPRECIATE AND VALUE OTHER'S IDEAS AND WORK

I Am Not a Picture . . .

I am a creation—the creation of an adventurous child who picked up a brush, and with bold strokes and brilliant colors, turned a blank piece of paper into a work of art with feelings and imagination. The child explored a new world, never giving thought to the masterpiece she created.

Soon she will have forgotten me, yet I was one of the many experiences that helped her grow.

I am not a picture.
I am a creation.
I am a child's painting.

Prayer

Dear Father in heaven, through the power of Your Holy Spirit, help me to give my children opportunities and time to use the many creative gifts You have given them.
Thank You for the gifts and talents You have granted our family. Help us to use them in service to You and others. Through Jesus our Lord. Amen.

EXPLORE, EXPERIMENT, CREATE

by Marti Beuschlein

I was the craftsman at His side. I was filled with delight day after day, rejoicing always in His presence, rejoicing in His whole world and delighting in mankind.

(Proverbs 8:30–31)

Play Dough Box

Fill a box with play dough, cookie cutters, rolling pin, potato masher, plastic knives, melon ball scoop, and other kitchen utensils.

Use this recipe for home-made play dough:

3 cups flour

1 ½ cups salt

3 tablespoons alum

3 tablespoons oil

2 ¼ cups water (add food coloring if desired)

Knead materials until well mixed. This may be kept for several weeks in a plastic bag or airtight container.

A Time to Create

Use plastic boxes to store art supplies. Have separate boxes for different media (i.e., one for play dough, one for painting, etc.). Pull out a box on a rainy day or when your children complain because they "don't have anything to do."

Art Box

Fill a box with blank paper, crayons, washable markers, glue sticks, stickers or sticky dots, colored paper, scissors, paper punch, masking tape, etc. The possibilities are endless.

Collage Box

Fill this box with a collection of bits and pieces of various materials.

Keep paper, glue, and scissors in the box along with pieces of gift wrap, greeting cards, ribbon, feathers, buttons, rickrack, sea shells, etc. (A paper plate without plastic coating is a good base for a collage.)

Paint Box

Fill this box with paintbrushes, (real paintbrushes from the hardware store are best), paint, paper, sponges cut into various shapes, a small plastic container to hold water, and a vinyl cloth or paper for covering the painting area.

Fun Recipes

Fun Finger Paint

Mix soap flakes (not powder) with water (begin with a small amount and add as needed).
Beat until the consistency of whipped cream, adding food coloring if desired. (It is better to add the food coloring to the water first.) Use an old-fashioned eggbeater and have your child help.

Sidewalk Chalk

Plaster of Paris

Small containers for molds (Styrofoam or Dixie cups, or Popsicle molds)

Water

Food coloring (if desired)

Put food coloring in water if desired.
Put Plaster of Paris into a small, throw-away container. Add water, stirring until the mixture resembles cake batter. Pour the mixture into molds and let set for at least two hours. Pop out chalk.

Gooey Goop

1 cup cornstarch
1 cup water
Food coloring

Put the ingredients into a large plastic bowl or dishpan and let your child mix away. Add more water each time it dries. Children grow and learn because of the many experiences they encounter in their development.
Art is one of these experiences—
an experience that is not to be taken lightly.

Prayer

Dear God, our gracious Creator, thank You for the wonderfully created children You have given to me. Help me to encourage their creativity as they explore Your world. In Jesus' name I pray. Amen.

SURE & TURE

by Marti Beuschlein

Let the earth be glad;
let the sea resound,
and all that is in it;
...they will sing
before the LORD.
(Psalm 96:11–13)

Listening to a babbling brook, or running sand through my fingers is soothing and comforting. In addition to the calming effect these activities have on children, playing with sand and water also serves as a foundation for learning math and science.

Children learn through sand and water play:

o THEY IMPROVE FINE MOTOR COORDINATION.

o THEY PRACTICE LANGUAGE AND SOCIAL SKILLS.

o THEY CAN EXPERIMENT WITH THE PHYSICAL PROPERTIES OF MATERIALS AS THEY MANIPULATE THE SAND AND WATER.

o THEY DEVELOP PROBLEM-SOLVING SKILLS.

o THEY LEARN ABOUT NATURAL ELEMENTS IN GOD'S WORLD.

Fun at Home

o COLLECT A VARIETY OF SAND AND WATER TOYS. PLASTIC SPRAY BOTTLES, EYE DROPPERS, SIEVES, SPONGES, PIECES OF HOSE OR PVC PIPE, BASTERS, FUNNELS, AND COMBS ARE ALL GREAT FOR SAND AND WATER PLAY. STORE THESE TOYS IN A PLASTIC BOX. THE BOX COULD ALSO BE USED AS A LARGE CONTAINER FOR HOLDING THE WATER OR SAND.

o MAKE FUNNELS FROM PLASTIC BOTTLES—CUT AROUND THE BOTTLE ABOUT THREE INCHES FROM THE OPENING. VARY THE BOTTLE SIZES FOR DIFFERENT EFFECTS WHEN POURING.

o CUT AN APRON FROM AN OILCLOTH OR VINYL TABLE-CLOTH TO PROTECT CLOTH-ING. (FOLD THE TABLECLOTH IN HALF, CUT A HOLE BIG ENOUGH TO SLIP OVER A CHILD'S HEAD, AND ADJUST THE WIDTH. HOLD THE SIDES TOGETHER WITH CLIP CLOTHESPINS.)

Dump and Spill

Set out two large, plastic containers, along with several plastic measuring cups. Put sand, cornmeal, rice, or water in one of the large containers. Encourage the children to fill measuring cups and pour them into the other large container.

Talk about how many cups it takes to fill the container. Feel the difference in weight when the cup is full and when it is empty. Give your children time to just experiment and enjoy the sand or water.

If your children are upset or having a bad day, use water in the large container —pouring water is very soothing for young children.

Sink and Float

Put water in a large container. Collect several items—a rock, an ice cube, Styrofoam trays, a spoon, a piece of aluminum foil— that sink or float. Drop the items into the water. Help your children observe whether each one sinks or floats.

Sort the items that sink into one pile and the items that float into another. Have your children try to guess whether each item will sink or float before dropping it in the water.

Language Enrichment

Enrich vocabulary by using these words as you and your children enjoy water/sand play: sink/float, dry/wet, more/less, change, dip, measure, pour, smooth/rough, patterns/designs, examine, and height/depth.

Prayer

Heavenly Father, through the power of Your Holy Spirit, give me the patience to teach my children about Your world—help me to show my children Your almighty power and love. In Jesus' name we pray. Amen.

Safety Precautions

Always put safety first when playing with water. Check the depth of the water to make sure it is not deep enough for your child to fall into. Be sure the containers you use are plastic or of another safe material. Never leave young children unattended near or in water.

Math—More Than Counting to Ten

by Marti Beuschlein

"Who endowed the heart with wisdom or gave understanding to the mind?
Who has the wisdom to count the clouds?" (Job 38:36–37)

"Nathan can count to 20!" my son Jonathan proudly told me. While this is quite an accomplishment for four-year-old Nathan, it is only a small part of understanding numbers and math. Counting by rote is actually memorizing the order of numbers and does not always indicate an actual understanding of the quantity of the numbers.

Young children do not learn math by listening to someone tell them about it—they learn by actually experiencing numbers.

Math is most certainly "hands-on" learning.

Teachers do many different activities to teach a comprehensive knowledge of math. These activities give the children "hands-on" opportunities to experience and discover math concepts. You may see children matching shapes, sorting objects according to size, shape or color, weighing pumpkins, measuring blocks, graphing likes and dislikes, or setting a table in the home center. All of these activities teach math.

Math Language Enrichment

Use these words with your children to enrich their vocabulary and understanding of math concepts:

Big/little, large/small, more/less, pounds/ounces, empty/full, first, second, third, last, tall/short, narrow/wide, circle, square, rectangle, triangle, oval, equal, and different

Fun at Home

You can build math foundations with everyday experiences. Try some of these activities at home.

Today Is Laundry Day

○ INVITE YOUR CHILDREN TO HELP YOU SORT THE LAUNDRY BY COLOR.

○ HAVE THEM POINT TO THE BIGGEST/SMALLEST PILE.

○ COMPARE DAD'S BIG SOCKS TO THEIR SMALL ONES.

○ COMPARE OTHER CLOTHING ITEMS.

○ LET YOUR CHILDREN PUT SOCKS IN PAIRS.

○ HELP YOUR CHILDREN MEASURE THE SOAP AND POUR IT INTO THE WASHING MACHINE.

○ HAVE THEM GUESS HOW MUCH WATER IS NEEDED TO COVER THE CLOTHES IN THE MACHINE.

○ HELP THEM LINE UP THE FOLDED CLOTHES ACCORDING TO SIZE.

Meal Time

○ HELP YOUR CHILDREN COUNT ENOUGH SILVERWARE AND DISHES FOR EVERYONE WHO WILL BE EATING.

○ HAVE THEM SET THE TABLE— PUTTING ONE PLATE, ONE GLASS, AND ONE OF EACH UTENSIL AT EACH PLACE.

○ TALK ABOUT THE DIFFERENT SHAPES OF FOOD AND/OR UTENSILS. "THESE PANS ARE CIRCLES, BUT THE CELERY IS A RECTANGLE."

○ HAVE YOUR CHILDREN OBSERVE THE FOOD AS IT COOKS. HOW DOES IT CHANGE? DOES IT GET BIGGER OR SMALLER?

Shopping

○ COMPARE CLOTHING OR FOOD SIZES. "ARE ALL APPLES RED?" "WHO WILL WEAR THIS TINY SHIRT?" "COUNT THE CANS I PUT INTO THE SHOPPING CART."

○ HAVE YOUR CHILDREN TELL YOU THE SHAPES OF CANS AND BOXES AS THEY HELP YOU PUT THEM AWAY.

Math Game

You will need dice and a deck of playing cards.

Roll the dice and count the number of dots. Pick up the same number of playing cards that matches the number on the dice. The person with the most cards is the winner. Play again and chart the results.

Prayer

Dear Lord, the task of parenting is awesome and overpowering. We are fearful of failing in this tremendously important task. Please help us to learn the way that is pleasing to You and a blessing to our family. Forgive us when we fail and keep our children in Your care. Be near us, Lord Jesus, as we pray. Amen.

DEVELOPMENTALLY APPROPRIATE

by Marti Beuschlein

So that your trust may be in the Lord, I teach you today ...
(Proverbs 22:19)

Developmentally appropriate programs provide children with time and experiences to help them grow according to their individual timetable— much like a plant.

A seed is planted in good dirt, watered, and given just the right amount of fertilizer so that it will grow and bloom into a beautiful flower. If given too much water or fertilizer, the plant will grow too fast, becoming tall and gangly or not grow at all.

It is the same with children. They need to bloom and grow naturally and in their own time. Pushing young children to learn beyond their developmental abilities produces the same results as the plant. As adults, we need to encourage and respect young children as they grow, develop, learn, discover, and experience God's world, His people, and His love.

"What is developmentally appropriate?"

my daughter-in-law called to ask. She was choosing a kindergarten for her son, and she had heard the term frequently.

Educators have learned through research that teaching practices for young children need to be developmentally appropriate.

That means that early childhood educators first think about the developmental needs of the children entrusted to them, then plan the curriculum and environment to meet the needs of those children. Such a program is planned to fit the needs of children, rather than fitting the children to the needs of a pre-planned program.

In a developmentally appropriate program you will see ...

o CHILDREN INITIATING THEIR OWN WORK AND PLAY.

o CHILDREN WHO ARE PHYSICALLY AND MENTALLY ACTIVE.

o CHILDREN WORKING IN SMALL GROUPS.

o CHILDREN MANIPULATING— TOUCHING AND FEELING— MATERIALS.

o CHILDREN EXHIBITING DIVERGENT THINKING— SOLVING THEIR OWN PROBLEMS.

o CHILDREN DISCOVERING, INVENTING, AND EXPERIENCING.

o TEACHERS ASKING INTERESTING QUESTIONS, SUPPLYING MATERIALS, PROVIDING A SUPPORTIVE AND INTERESTING ENVIRONMENT, AND ENCOURAGING CHILDREN TO GROW AND LEARN.

Prayer

Dear Jesus, help me to consider my children as given to me by You. Forgive me when I expect too much from them or let my ego become too involved in their success. Help me to realize this and to encourage them to grow and learn in their own time. Thank You, Lord. Amen.

HANDS-ON-LEARNING

by Marti Beuschlein

Reflect on what I am saying, for the Lord will give you insight into all this. (2 Timothy 2:7)

A parent asked me this question as the director of the early childhood program: "Why are the children always moving around and why they are so noisy? How can they be learning?" My answer was simple: "Active children means active learning."

We know through research that young children learn best by using all their senses—touching, smelling, tasting, hearing, and seeing. They love to explore, move, discover, and interact with each other. As they do this, they grow and learn. The more experiences and "hands-on" activities provided, the more the children are learning.

Children need ...

o TO BE TRUSTED TO ENGAGE IN INTERESTING ACTIVITIES.

o OPPORTUNITIES TO DISCOVER ON THEIR OWN.

o OPPORTUNITIES TO FIND AND EXPLORE THEIR OWN INTERESTS.

o OPPORTUNITIES TO SOCIALIZE WITH FRIENDS.

o THE GIFT OF HANDS-ON EXPERIENCES.

My friend Bev Beckman once said, "What can I give my children today? Only a morsel of meal, or a day full of experiences with touching, seeing, tasting, smelling, and hearing? How can I help my children feel and understand God's love unless I demonstrate that love by being the best-possible, most-loving teacher? Then my hands will be full of meal and He who gives all will bless my life."

I could not have said it better. Enjoy a "day full of experiences" with your children.

Fun at Home

Save That Junk Mail

Give junk mail to your children along with a pencil, scissors, tape, and perhaps an old purse or briefcase.
Turn them loose and watch what happens.

Sidewalk Fun

Give your children a bucket of water, some chalk (the bigger the better), and old paint-brushes. Have them use the chalk and water to draw/paint pictures on the sidewalk. Ask "What happened to the water after you painted a picture? Where did it go?" "Does the chalk look different when it's wet?" Step back and watch them discover.

Down the Tube

You will need an empty paper-towel or gift-wrap tube, and a ball (or anything else round that will roll down the tube). Include some items that will not roll easily. Let your children experiment with different ways and things to roll down the tube.

We Remember:

10% of what we hear,

50% of what we see,

70% of what we say,

90% of what we DO.

Prayer

Dear God, there is so much to do and learn. Grant me the wisdom to absorb it and put this new knowledge into action. I trust in Your strength and care. Thank You for Your love and patience. In Jesus' name. Amen.